PRAYER GALLERY

A CREATIVE, ACCESSIBLE, AND FUN WAY TO ENGAGE WITH PRAYER

ELEANOR KING

DAN PIERCE

First Published in 2023 by Kevin Mayhew Ltd,
Fengate Farm,
Rattlesden,
Bury St Edmunds,
Suffolk, IP30 0SZ

Copyright © 2023 Eleanor King & Dan Pierce

ISBN (paperback): 9781838581558
ISBN (eBook): 9781838581565
Paperback product code: 1501728
eBook product code: 1501729

Scripture quotations are from New Revised Standard Version Bible: Anglicized Edition, copyright © 1989, 1995 National Council of the of the Churches of Christ in the United States of America. Used by permission.
All rights reserved worldwide.

THE HOLY BIBLE, NEW INTERNATIONAL VERSION®, NIV® Copyright © 1973, 1978, 1984, 2011 by Biblica, Inc.® Used by permission.
All rights reserved worldwide.

No part of this book may be reproduced in any form or by any electronic or mechanical means, including information storage and retrieval systems, without written permission from the author, except for the use of brief quotations in a book review.

CONTENTS

Introduction	v
1. Time	1
2. Light	6
3. Rebuilding, restoring and repairing	11
4. Endings and Beginnings	16
5. Habits / rhythms	21
6. Water	27
7. Unity	33
8. Playfulness	39
9. Reflections	44
10. Justice / equality	50
11. Listening and noticing	56
12. Climate and environment	61

INTRODUCTION

Imagine what we might hope for in a comfortable family gathering — perhaps at Christmas, or for another special celebration. Spending the day together – well, kind of together – in each other's company, but often doing very different things. One person might be sitting reading the paper. Others might be watching a movie. Siblings might be bickering, in a friendly sort of way. Grandad might sleep, and the cousins might play board games. Everyone continually topped up with food and drink. All together, completely together, yet occupied in all sorts of different ways.

Think about any kind of space like this, and you will be close to what we have in mind in this book. Although, of course, people's experiences of Christmas and other family gatherings may have been painful or difficult, as a church family we have the opportunity and privilege of being able to offer a friendly, welcoming, and inclusive space where people can connect in a meaningful and creative way with God and with each other. We can encourage creating community gatherings where everyone is at liberty to choose how they engage. These spaces

INTRODUCTION

respect the interests and energies of young and old all under one roof – kind of like a gallery.

If you have ever been to an art gallery, you will have wandered among exhibits, some of which may have moved you and others which may have left you cold. It is unlikely, however, that at least one picture or installation will not have affected you in some way – provoked, inspired, charmed, or confused. With our galleries, we look to create a similar experience. In this book, we offer a range of creative, thought-provoking and interactive ideas to engage those who gather in prayer. Everybody is different, so variety is key – our beautiful, God-created human diversity is an asset rather than a problem. What touches one person may completely bypass the next. When visiting an art gallery or exhibition with a friend, we may find that we appreciate very contrasting artwork, with one of us pointing to a piece we like only to discover the other does not. So when curating these spaces, it is good to offer as much diversity as possible.

As well as offering different, creative, and inclusive ways for people who already attend church to pray and reflect, prayer galleries can also be a really accessible way for those who are not familiar with church to explore prayer and spirituality. The prayer stations could be used in a church setting, in a hall, outdoors, in a school, at home, or even at a cafe. The flexible and open-ended approach provides the opportunity for people to connect with God and with each other in a way and at a pace that works for them. We have tried to ensure that all activities can be set up using readily accessible resources, and have offered alternatives where appropriate. Some people might like to pick and choose a few different prayer stations to suit their setting, while others might like to use all six, based on a particular theme. We hope that the book may also lead people to come up with some of their own wonderful and creative ideas, and we would love to hear about these too!

INTRODUCTION

A FEW PRACTICAL CONSIDERATIONS

When planning your prayer gallery, it is good to take into account the ages of those who may be attending, as well as any allergies, physical or learning disabilities, or other conditions that may affect how people are able to interact with the different stations.

In some cases, it may be a good idea to adapt the activities a little, to think of the position of each prayer station to make sure that it is accessible but also safe, and to consider having someone keep an eye on certain stations, such as those involving scissors, food, paint, or marker pens!

CHAPTER 1
TIME

An opportunity to think together about how God is with us in the past, present, and future, make space to rest in God's presence, and reflect on how thankfulness can be part of our prayers throughout the day.

GOD IS ALWAYS WITH US

Bring along some objects of different ages, such as some tickets or receipts, an old mug or plate, some buttons, some stones, a postcard, a book, a piece of brick or tile, and a twig or stick from a tree. Also prepare some pieces of paper or card with these words on: 'This week – God is with us', 'This year -- God is with us', 'This century – God is with us', 'Over thousands of years – God is with us'. People can then look at, pick up, and explore the objects and place them in the different categories, remembering that God is with us in the past, present and years to come.

TREE RING REFLECTION

Either bring a picture or an actual log of wood where the inner rings can be clearly seen. Place the log on the floor with cushions around it. Next to the log, write a prompt that asks participants to count the rings, each representing a year in the life of the tree. The thickness and shade of the rings give clues to the health or otherwise of the tree in any particular year. It will have enjoyed and endured both good and bad times. Encourage participants to consider their own years of growth with a simple prayer:

'Take Lord, and receive into your care, all the years that have passed and all the years yet to come. Amen'

THANKFUL PRAYERS AROUND THE CLOCK

Lay an analogue clock in the middle of a large sheet of paper or card. Using a marker pen, draw around the edge of it. Next, divide the surrounding card into twelve equal portions, corresponding to the hour sections on the clock, but radiating out in a sunshine-like pattern. At the top of the piece of paper or card, write the words 'At all times of day, we thank you, Lord'. Provide some different coloured marker pens so that people can write down things that they are thankful for at different times of the day, writing some yourself first, as an example.

PRAYER GALLERY

THANKFUL PRAYERS AROUND THE CLOCK

A HEART OF LOVE

Find as big a piece of cardboard as you can and cut it into a heart shape. Paint it red, or cover it with red paper. Find a place in your prayer gallery venue where this can be prominent; it can be very striking as people enter the space. Write out an instruction card with these words:
'First, find your pulse, either in your wrist or on your neck. Be very conscious of your own heartbeat, and pray that it may beat in time with God's, racing with the things that animate God's heart, and at other times simply finding your resting rhythm with God's.'
Keep the heart, as you can use it again with different instructions –or just have it as a decoration for future galleries.

TIME TO REST

Create a comfortable area for people to sit for a while, with cushions and blankets on the floor. Place a 1 or 2-minute sand timer (or a sensory timer where coloured liquid trickles down) on a tray covered in foil with stones around it. Write the words 'Take a minute or two to rest in God's company' on a piece of paper or card and place this in front of the timer.

A TIME FOR EVERYTHING

Write out a section from Ecclesiastes 3:1-8 in an interesting and creative way – perhaps using paint or stencils on a piece of wood, cross-stitch or embroidery on a large embroidery hoop made from a child's hula hoop covered in fabric from an old sheet, or perhaps calligraphy or colourful collage on a large piece of card. Make the wording large enough so that it can be seen from a few paces away. The passage is fairly long, so choose a few verses to focus on:

'For everything there is a season, and a time for every matter under heaven: a time to be born, and a time to die; a time to plant, and a time to pluck up what is planted; a time to kill, and a time to heal; a time to break down, and a time to build up; a time to weep, and a time to laugh; a time to mourn and a time to dance; a time to throw away stones, and a time to gather stones together; a time to embrace and a time to refrain from embracing; a time to seek, and a time to lose; a time to keep, and a time to throw away; a time to tear, and a time to sew; a time to keep silence, and a time to speak; a time to love, and a time to hate; a time for war, and a time for peace.' (Ecclesiastes 3:1-8, NRSVA).

CHAPTER 2
LIGHT

Create a light display to help pray for the world, use what we know about light to help us think about Jesus as the Light of the World, and reflect on the way God's light and goodness can shine in our lives.

INVISIBLE INK BLESSINGS

Using invisible pens (which show up when UV light shines on them, such as those used for marking bikes with a postcode), write messages of God's love and hope inside some cards. These could include things such as 'God wants to hear your story', 'God cares about you', 'God likes you and knows how precious you are'. As people visit the prayer station, they can read the secret messages hidden in the cards using the UV light on the end of one of the pens. Leave some other cards blank in a pile for people to add their own messages of God's kindness and care for others to find. In case people have never used spy pens or invisible ink before, leave some instructions by the prayer station explaining what to do. If you can't find any UV pens, then lemon juice will do the same job. Use a small paintbrush to write short messages with the lemon juice 'ink' on white paper (not card this time) and provide a torch so that people can see the message when they hold it up to the light.

LIGHT OF THE WORLD

Write in large print on a big piece of card lots of facts about light, such as: light travels in a straight line; objects in its path cause light to bend or refract; the speed of light is exactly 299,792km per second; travelling at the speed of light, you could go around the earth 7.5 times in a second; light travels faster than sound; light from the sun takes just over 8 minutes to travel the 93 million miles from the Sun to the Earth! Ask participants to reflect on these facts in view of what Jesus says about himself in John 8:12 – 'I am the light of the world. Whoever follows me will never walk in darkness but will have the light of life' (NRSVA). Depending on your group, it may also be helpful to provide some shiny star stickers for younger community members to decorate the card.

MILK BOTTLE LIGHT DISPLAY

Create a light display by hanging up empty milk bottles on a string. Put battery-operated LED strings of lights, or small LED keyring torches inside them, so that they light up. Provide glue sticks, coloured tissue paper, and permanent marker pens for people to decorate the light display with different colours as they pray: white for those places and situations in need of peace, greens and blues for our world with its forests and oceans, and pinks or reds for the people and circumstances in need of God's love. Start off the prayers by writing the words

'Lord, bring your light in places which need peace', 'Lord, bring your light to the earth we share', 'Lord, bring your light to all those in need of your love'. People can then use the permanent marker pens to add their own words of prayer onto the milk bottles.

MILK BOTTLE LIGHT DISPLAY

LIGHT BULB REFLECTION

Tape an A3 piece of black card firmly onto a table top. Find some bulbs of different shapes and sizes– such as a torch bulb, lamp bulb, or bicycle light. Using large blobs of sticky tack (black coloured if possible), fix the bulbs in place so that they are standing upwards. Write a card with the following words as an aid to reflection:

'Different shapes. Different potential outputs. But all must be attached to a power source.'

SEE THE LIGHT SHINE THROUGH

Collect various items which look different when light is shone on them - for example, pieces of glass smoothed by the sea, amber or tree resin, beads from old jewellery, glass shapes or marbles, an old lampshade, coloured plastic beakers, bowls or plates. Provide a torch or two, or a couple of LED tealights, so that people can explore the objects and see how the light transforms them. In between the objects, write out these short prayers using permanent marker pens on pieces of coloured cellophane or tissue paper:

'Lord Jesus, may your love shine in my life', 'Thank you, Lord, for your light', 'Loving God, you bring light in the darkness' and 'Jesus, you are the light of the world'.

MAKING SHADOWS

This one needs daylight and a decent window, or a well-placed lamp. Use masking tape to fix a card saying 'stand here' onto the floor. Set it up so that someone could stand on that spot and see all or most of their body as a shadow image on the wall or ground. Write a few words as an aid to reflection:

'God's light surrounds us, protects us, encourages us, and strengthens us. May our actions be lit up with his love. Amen'

CHAPTER 3
REBUILDING, RESTORING AND REPAIRING

Take time to receive God's healing and restoration through creativity and prayer; bring to God those places in our community in need of rebuilding; and think about how we can reuse and repair the things we have to reduce waste and care for the environment.

JIGSAW BLESSINGS

Find three or four greeting cards or postcards with attractive landscape scenes on them. Use a marker pen to carefully add some words of prayer to the pictures (written over the picture itself), such as 'May you know God's healing love', 'May you be filled with God's grace' and 'May you know God's wisdom and care'. Next, cut each picture into pieces, creating some small jigsaws, and place each of these on a tray. While putting together the jigsaw puzzles, people can piece together the beautiful scenes of God's creation and read the words of God's blessings and promises.

JIGSAW BLESSINGS

RENEWAL AND REPAIR IN OUR COMMUNITY

Take a walk around your neighbourhood, or go further and walk around your village, town, or city. Are there any run-down buildings, rusted signs, potholes, or anything else in clear sign of disrepair? Take some photos, where appropriate, and create a display using these pictures. It's particularly helpful if at least some of this dilapidated infrastructure has the quality of being well known – local landmarks that have perhaps seen better days . Write out these words as an aid to prayer:

'Lord, we bring before you these things in need of renewal and repair, and pray for the community of people who live and work there. Help us to make a difference so that we can bring hope, healing, and new life'.

Provide some sticky notes for people to add ideas for positive actions that could make a difference.

FOIL COLLAGE

On a couple of trays, place some colourful pieces of foil, such as those that come wrapped around some chocolates or sweets (or with the chocolates still inside, for people to eat first!). Cut out a large heart shape from card, with some glue sticks next to this. Encourage people to spend some time smoothing out the foil carefully before glueing it onto the heart to make a shiny and colourful collage. Write out this prayer for people to use as they smooth out the pieces of foil:

'Lord Jesus, we come just as we are. Sometimes confused, sometimes anxious, sometimes afraid. Thank you for the way you reassure us, heal us, and comfort us. Amen'

REPAIRING BEAUTIFULLY

The Japanese art of kintsugi (golden repair) or kintsukuroi (golden joinery) is a pottery repair method that has been practised for over 400 years. Instead of discarding broken artefacts this practice honours their unique history by emphasising, not hiding, the break. This is now a commonly used metaphor to describe how the process of healing from our hurt may powerfully change us. Sometimes in the process of repairing things that have broken, we create something more unique, resilient, and even beautiful. This may remind us of the resurrected Christ appearing to the disciples and revealing his scars. If this would be appropriate for your group, set out the items from a kintsugi kit (available online or from a craft shop) so that people can have a go at repairing the bowls provided in a beautiful way. A more low-tech and family-friendly version could be to cut some postcards into pieces for people to reassemble on another piece of card, glueing them in place with small gaps between the pieces. A gold pen can then be used to colour in the gaps, producing a beautiful and interesting piece of artwork. Write out this prayer for people to use as they take part in the craft activity:

'Loving God, you know us inside and out. You know the good things – and the tough things that have happened in our lives. We bring them all before you and ask that, as we pray, you heal us and mend us with your love and grace. Amen'

MAKE A CROSS FROM SMOOTH STICKS

Bring along some sticks or small pieces of wood, as well as some sheets of sandpaper and some string. Place these on a large sheet or old curtain, to catch the sawdust. People can choose a couple of sticks and sand them down to make them smooth. Write out this prayer for people to use, if they choose to, while they do this:

'Loving God, I bring to you the things in my life that are rough and spiky, splintery, or prickly. Thank you for the way you smooth them out with your love. Amen'

After this, people can tie two sticks together with the string to create a cross, winding it around the front and back several times before tying the ends together in a knot.

FRUIT THAT WILL LAST

Earnest Elmo Calkins is seen as the father of modern marketing and advertising. In the early 1930s he coined the term 'planned obsolescence' which encourages the production of goods that are no longer made to last. Why? Because if things wear out quickly, customers must return again and again to purchase replacements, therefore maximising profits. This became known as 'consumer engineering', locking shoppers into a rapid cycle of acquisition and waste. For this Prayer Gallery installation, gather as many broken electrical goods as you can –old phones, hairdryers, computers, TVs, garden tools, or kitchen appliances. Display these in a pile. This piece is entitled, 'Fruit that will last?' Copy the above introduction to Calkin's ideas onto card beneath the title, along with the following prayer:

'Lord, help us to be aware of what we buy and what we use, finding ways to reduce, reuse, recycle, and repair. We commit ourselves to responsible stewardship of all creation. Amen'

CHAPTER 4
ENDINGS AND BEGINNINGS

An opportunity to think about how God is with us in the endings and beginnings in our lives, and to reflect on where God may be leading us in the future.

JAM JAR REFLECTION

Bring along some jars of jam in various stages of being eaten. Also bring along a clean, empty jar, and one that is full (preferably homemade, in a re-used jar. If you don't have home-made jam, then take the label off a new jar of jam). Place these in a circle on a piece of fabric or tablecloth - perhaps a checked, picnic style one if you have it. Put them in order of fullness, so that they show the life cycle of a jam jar– from empty, to full, and then slowly being used up until the jam is gone again, when the jar can be washed and reused. Place a loaf of bread in the middle of the jar circle. In front of the loaf of bread, display this prayer:

'Lord, thank you for being with us at the beginnings, the endings,

and in between. Just as the jam tastes just as good at the top of the jar as it does at the bottom, help us to know and share the sweetness of your love at every stage of our lives. Thank you for your hope that encourages us, your peace that surrounds us, and your love that never ends. Amen'

JAM JAR REFLECTION

OPENING LINE OF A NOVEL

The opening line of a book has a very important function. The customer in a bookshop picks up a novel and flicks through it, perhaps pausing to read. That opening line has to arrest them, draw them in, engulf them, and enthuse them to continue. That opening line must compel the reader to buy into the story. Pride and Prejudice, Harry Potter, 1984, Moby Dick, and many more all grab the reader with their openings. Print some opening lines from famous stories like these on separate bits of card. Include Genesis 1, John 1, and perhaps another Bible book of your choosing. On another set of cards, print the title of the book from which you have taken the quotes. Present these cards laid out but not in order, scattered around. Participants can try to match the book title with the correct quote – have an answers sheet face down so they can check their answers when they have finished. Also provide some plain card and a pen so that once participants have correctly matched the quotes, they can write down their own 'opening line' as the start of a prayer for the week ahead.

LAST LINE OF THE CHORUS

The first line of a song and the last line of a song's chorus are vital. The first line must draw the listener in, and the last line should have the quality of staying in their mind. This is also often used as the song's title. Provide some Bibles in different translations, with a bookmark placed at the Psalms, as well as some squares of card, and some colourful pens. Write out these instructions for people to follow as they take part in this activity:

Think about the catchy last line of one of your favourite songs.

Look through the Psalms – the Bible's own songbook –and find a line of a Psalm that would make a catchy song title or the last line at the end of a song's chorus. Choose something that resonates with how you think or feel right now. Using the card and pens provided, colourfully write your Psalm sentence as if you are creating artwork for its release as a single. The finished artworks can be displayed together as an aid to worship and prayer.

MARBLE RUN

Set up a marble run on a large tray to prevent marbles rolling over the floor. Provide a variety of colourful marbles in a pot. As people choose a marble, and it rolls its way down the slopes to the bottom, this prayer can be used:

'Loving God, show us the things in our life that are just beginning, the things that are ending, and those things that are somewhere in between. We bring all these into your caring, comforting, and healing presence. Amen'

RECYCLING LIFE CYCLE

Create a few piles of recyclable materials, such as some plastic bottles, some old paper or card, and some cans. Perhaps put aside your household recycling for a few weeks to create various impressive piles of recyclable materials, or ask another member of your community to collect things. You might like to stack these up or arrange them in interesting ways so that they are particularly eye-catching within your gallery. Write out these words to encourage people to reflect on the future of the items: 'Think about what materials these items came from, what they have been used for, and what they might become'. Next to the piles of recycling, display this prayer:

'Loving God, you have walked with us in our past. Although some things have come to an end, we are glad that you look forward to walking through the future with us. Amen'

LIFE AND GROWTH

Collect some pieces of wood on which the grain or rings show – smooth, sanded, or polished pieces that feel good to touch. Arrange these on a table or piece of fabric so that people can pick up the ones that appeal to them, hold them, and look at them. Write out these words of prayerful reflection:

'From a tiny seed, a sapling grew. The rain fell, the seasons changed, and the sun shone. The sapling became stronger and taller. Its branches spread out, and as a mature tree, it soaked up the sunshine. Its roots reached far down underground to collect the water it needed to grow. It was a home for creatures, big and small, and provided shade and shelter. The unique grain in the wood and the many tree rings we can see show the story of this life and growth, now so beautiful, but in a different way. We give thanks for all life, and all creation. In the beginnings, in the growth, and in the endings, God is there'.

CHAPTER 5
HABITS / RHYTHMS

A chance to use our creativity to make things that help us remember to pray, with thought-provoking prayer starters and reflections to kick-start our prayer life in a new way.

LOOKING THROUGH GOD'S EYES

You will need a piece of A4 paper or card, rolled into a 4cm tube and taped in place, and two cocktail sticks. Make a small hole about three quarters of the way along your tube with the cocktail stick and push it right through so that it can be seen on the other side. Do the same with the second cocktail stick so as to create a cross shape inside the tube. When you look down the tube, it should now look a bit like the view through a telescope. Once participants have made their device, they are invited to look through it– at their hands, their feet, their friends, and their surroundings. The following prayer may be said:

'I look at all things and places, and people through the lens of the cross, pondering its power. May my vision be shaped by Christ's love,

my eyes be led by Christ's purpose, and each new image be a target for the outworking of his grace.'

LOOKING THROUGH GOD'S EYES

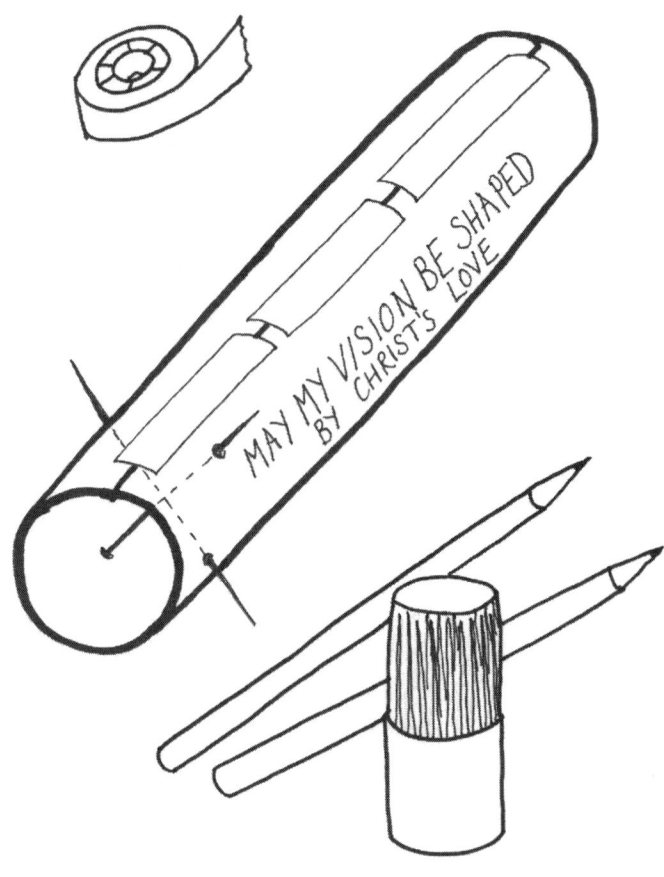

MAY MY VISION BE SHAPED BY CHRIST'S LOVE

PRAYER BRACELETS

Bring along some stretchy bracelet elastic (or cord) and some different-coloured beads, made from various materials. People can make their own prayer bracelet as a way of getting into the habit of prayer in the spare corners of time when there is a quiet moment. First, tie a bead securely with a double knot onto the end of a 30 cm piece of elastic. Add more beads in different colours to serve as a reminder to pray for different things, with suggestions written on a card:

'Brown for the earth, green for forests and all who live in them, blue for the seas and oceans, white for peace, pink for love and reconciliation, orange for hope, purple for holiness, and yellow for joy. People can thread the beads onto the elastic in the order and combination that they would like, and then, when the bracelet is large enough, they can tie the ends of the elastic securely together. The first bead that was tied on will be slightly separated from the others. This can be the start and end bead, so that people can use the prayer beads without having to look and just by feeling where they have reached the end of the circle.'

COLLAGE PRAYER COASTERS

Using some card, colourful paper, pictures of landscapes, and a few photocopied pages with encouraging words from scripture, people can create their own coasters as an aid to prayer whenever they have a cup of tea or coffee, helping create a habit of prayer at this time. First of all, cut out some circles of thick card, a bit larger than a mug. Provide some colourful paper, pages from magazines showing plants, flowers, and natural landscapes, some photocopied prayers or psalms, some scissors, glue sticks, and some sticky backed plastic or sticky tape. People can decorate their cardboard coaster by glueing on pieces of paper and words that mean something to them, and then protect the coaster from spilt tea or coffee by covering it with sticky-backed plastic or some strips of sticky tape.

PRAYER KEYRING

People can make a keyring to add to their keys as a reminder to pray. Bring along some pieces of felt, some sharp scissors, some needles and embroidery thread, and some PVA glue with glue spreaders (for people who would prefer not to sew). Create an example for people to follow by cutting out a simple small house shape from three layers of felt. You can add a small door and windows from felt scraps too, and either sew these on to the top layer or stick them on with glue. Either glue the layers together or use the needle and thread to stitch firmly around the edge. Finally, thread a needle with a length of embroidery silk and push this through the felt, near the point of the roof of the house. Repeat this several times, so that there are a few loops together at the top of the house. Tie the two ends of this piece of thread together securely. This loop can be used to attach the house to a set of keys. Write out this prayer for people to think of when they use their keys:

'Lord God, thank you that our home is always with you. May we make space in our lives and our homes for your love and presence every day. Amen'

SONGLINES

This activity may be done individually or corporately

(whichever is more appropriate for your setting). The following text can be used as an introduction:

'Within Indigenous Australian culture, there exists a means of navigation called The Songlines. The Songlines are traditional stories, songs, art, and dance about rock, bush, waterholes, stars, and other natural phenomena that help people track across the vast outback. No road signs, no trail of hand-laid pointers. Instead, journeys are mapped by singing their people's story.

These Songlines are not only territorial markers but also powerful sources of corporate memory and identity. If they were written down, they would fill libraries, and yet they are not written down –they are simply sung from one generation to the next. Huge amounts of intricate knowledge are remembered only through melody and rhythm, enabling the traveller to journey vast distances without so much as a map or compass.

Similar traditions span the ages and cultures of our world. The book of Psalms in the Bible belongs to this vibrant heritage. A people's story transported aurally long before it was written down. One of these ancient songwriters wrote, "Sing to the Lord a new song". It's a refrain used throughout the Psalms and an encouragement to continue storytelling as life unfolds. Similar to the indigenous Aussies, The Psalmist is asking us to use song as a means of corporate memory and identity formation.

Thinking either of your personal story or that of your group, use a large roll of paper to create an illustrated timeline of your individual life or your life together. Write out these prompts on the paper in thought bubbles:

'What features will you consciously remember as warnings or encouragements that tell your history?'
'What songs, books, film or art have been influential in your life?'

'What particular life events have shaped who you are becoming?'
'What verses from Scripture have been like landmarks along your way?'
'What people have been significant?'
'What symbols might you use to represent aspects of this narrative?"

PRAYER STARTERS

It can be quite normal for us to begin our prayers with whatever easily comes to mind. Perhaps our own circumstances or some particular person, place or desire. However, this next prayer station is designed to challenge us with an alternative starting point for prayer. It is designed to jog our imaginations and stir unexpected responses from us. For this station, you will need to create four lists. Write a list of themes like hope, generosity, hospitality, friendship, loyalty, patience, and honesty. Then write a list of places, for example: bus station, Kenya, cafe, prison, supermarket, New Zealand, hotel, farm, bank, court, etc. Next, write a list of characters, such as: grandad, police officer, queen, monkey, judge, author, surfer, teacher, poet, doctor, parrot, pop star etc. Finally write a list of objects: book, phone, teapot, egg, spade, banana, picture frame, biscuit tin, bicycle pump etc. Cut your lists into individual words, which are then folded up and each list placed in separate containers that are labelled: themes, places, characters, and objects.

The idea is both simple and yet challenging. Write out these instructions:

'Pick a folded word from one of the four containers of your choosing. This will provide a theme, place, character, and an object. You are invited to prayerfully think about these, asking yourself two questions:'What does this word mean to me? What might this word cause me to pray?"

CHAPTER 6
WATER

Activities to help us reflect on God's gift of water, use our senses to explore water in a prayerful way, pray for the watery places in the world, and think about the symbolism of water in our own prayer lives.

ROSE OF JERICHO

Print the following information next to two pictures of the plant it describes, along with an actual plant if you have one (available to buy online for a few pounds). One picture needs to show it in drought conditions, the other picture in bloom:

'The Rose of Jericho is a plant native to western Asia. This small, hardy grey plant can withstand extraordinary dry spells. In sustained dry conditions, it curls its branches and seedpods inward, forming a ball that opens only when moistened. If uprooted, it blows around as tumbleweed. The famous songwriter Paul Simon adopts it for his visceral depiction of grief in the song 'The Coast' on his 1991 album 'The Rhythm of the Saints'. If still rooted, this extraordinary

little plant offers us a beautiful image of hope. It can survive drought for years curled up, desiccated, withered, and lifeless. Even after sustained malnourishment, when it is given just a little water, it will begin to flourish. It spreads into a large, green plant as much as a foot wide, bearing tiny white flowers. You can watch this on a video online; just type in 'Rose of Jericho', and watch a time-lapse clip of one coming back to life. The alternative name for the Rose of Jericho is 'The Resurrection Plant'. At times, our faith can feel dried up, and the way back to God seems impossibly hard. Remember the words of Moses in Deuteronomy 31:6: "the LORD your God goes with you; he will never leave you nor forsake you."'

WATER TASTING

Bring along some different waters for people to try, including tap water, sparkling water, spring water, boiled water, and flavoured water. Provide some cups so that people can try a little of each of them. Using a large sheet of card, create a tasting chart by writing the names of the different types of waters on the left and leaving space for people to write their comments on the right. Write out these instructions on a second piece of card for people to read as they engage with the activity:

'Taste a little of each of the different types of water. Take time to notice the temperature, the flavour, and the feel of the water. Record your thoughts on the tasting chart, in thankfulness to God for the water we drink every day.'

PRAYER GALLERY

WATER TASTING

PAPER WATERLILIES

Bring along a large, shallow bowl or a deep tray, some small (8-10cm) squares of coloured paper, some scissors, and some pens. Fill the bowl or tray with water. Cut out a paper waterlily as an example for others to follow, and write out these instructions:

'First, take a square of coloured paper. Fold this diagonally in half, and then in half again. Cut around the open edge to create a petal shape. Next, open the paper flower. Fold each petal over and over a few times towards the inside of the flower. Carefully place your waterlily to float in the tray, and watch while it gradually opens up.'
Write out this prayer for people to use as they watch their flower open:

'Loving God, thank you for the way you give us rest and refreshment. Help us to open up to receive your love. Amen'

POURING WATER

It can be very relaxing to watch moving water, such as a waterfall, river, sea, or rainstorm. However, small-scale moving water can also be a helpful aid to reflection and is quite beautiful in its own way. Bring along a few large tubs, such as washing-up bowls or buckets, as well as some jugs for pouring. Also bring some children's bath toys or water play toys if you have them, such as small sieves, water mills, and toy teapots. Place these on the floor on some large old towels to catch the drips. Write out this prayer and tape it to the washing-up bowls and buckets:

'Lord God, as we pour this beautiful water, we are reminded of your generosity, your grace, and your love. Thank you for the water you give us. Help us to appreciate it and look after the watery places you have made. Amen'

WATERCOLOUR WASH

Bring along some sets of watercolour paints (the solid tablet sort), some large and small brushes, some white paper (either watercolour paper or ordinary A4 printer paper), and some jars or containers of water. Write out these instructions and make an example version for others to follow too:

'First, use a large brush to paint water all over your paper. Next, use a small brush to add some colour by rubbing the brush gently on the watercolour tablets and then drawing the paintbrush across the wet paper. This could be for a background or a landscape, or just some more abstract patches of colour that appeal to you. As you add the colour, watch how the water helps it spread over the page, in the same way that our small offerings of kindness can spread much further than we expect, through God's love and grace.'

ICE AND WATER

Prepare a few blocks of ice before the event by freezing water in some plastic containers. If you have not had time to do this, a bag of ice from the shop will also work well. Place the ice in a large tub, such as a washing-up bowl or large mixing bowl, and provide some jugs of hot water, either from the hot tap or from the kettle, safely diluted with cold tap water to a hand-hot temperature. Write out this prayer for people to use as they slowly melt the ice by pouring hot water over it:

'Loving God, sometimes we feel frozen in sadness or feel we are not good enough. Thank you that as we spend time in your kind and caring presence, we can experience the warmth of your love, pouring over us, surrounding us, and healing us. Amen'

CHAPTER 7
UNITY

Prayerfully work together to create some community artwork and solve some puzzles with the help of others, while reflecting on words from scripture on the theme of unity.

WEAVING TOGETHER

Set up a simple weaving loom using a couple of large rectangles of corrugated cardboard, glued together. At the top and at the bottom, cut a series of 1 cm deep slits, each 1 cm apart. These will hold the wool in place. Using a ball of wool, tie one end securely in place to the first slit at the top of the cardboard. Next, wind the wool around the cardboard, from the top to the bottom, then around the back of the loom, over the top again and through the second slit, down from the top to the bottom again, and so on. When you get to the last slit in the cardboard, cut the wool and tie it on. Bring along a variety of different wool, string and thread, as well as some large plastic needles (such as the sort children use for learning to sew, or for sewing up knitted items). People can choose some thread that they like, and use this to add a section to the communal piece of weaving. Write these words of prayer clearly on the cardboard loom:

'Lord God, thank you that you have made us all different– help us to work together through your love. Amen'

COMMUNITY CANVAS

Bring along a large canvas on a wooden frame (a simple and low cost one is fine), some felt tip pens, and a couple of permanent marker pens (a shiny or metallic colour if possible, but any colour will work). Using a permanent marker pen, draw a winding line all over the canvas, creating random spaces formed by the lines crossing over each other. People can participate in the activity by colouring in a section with a felt tip pen and then using a permanent marker pen to write a word that they think expresses what they like about being part of this community. Start the artwork off with one or two examples of your own.

HANDPRINT COLLAGE

Bring along some different coloured and patterned pieces of paper, some pencils, some scissors, some glue sticks, and a large piece of card, cut into the shape of a heart. In the middle of the cardboard heart, draw a small heart using a permanent marker pen, and write these words inside: 'Thank you God for making us different, and thank you for loving us just the same'. Each person can draw around their hand on a piece of paper they choose, cut this out, and then stick it on to the cardboard heart shape using the glue stick.

SOLVING THE PUZZLES TOGETHER

On three large, colourful pieces of cardboard, write out the words from these Bible passages, using permanent marker pens:

'By this everyone will know that you are my disciples, if you have love for one another' (John 13:35 NRSVA)

'Make every effort to keep the unity of the Spirit through the bond of peace' (Ephesians 4:3 NIV)

'How good and pleasant it is when God's people live together in unity!' (Psalm 133:1 NRSVA)

Cut up the boards into pieces, like a jigsaw, using a craft knife or some large, strong scissors. Mix these up and place the pieces in a few shopping bags, which you can hide around your venue. Ask people to have a look for the bags and bring them back. As a group activity, people can piece the puzzles together so that the verses can be read out loud. Then, in pairs, people can practise learning the passages until they can remember them by heart. Invite participants to take a photo of the completed puzzles so that they can continue to reflect on them during the week.

PAPER CIRCLE OF FRIENDSHIP

Fold some squares of paper diagonally into eight, similar to the start of the process when making a paper snowflake. This will give you a triangular wedge shape. Place this so that the point of the triangle is facing you. On this triangle, use a pencil to draw the outline of a person, with their feet touching the folded edges each side of the point of the triangle, their arms further up, reaching out and touching the folded edges at the side, and their head near the cut edge of the paper at the top. Cut carefully around the edge of one of the figures, through all the paper layers, so that when you open out the paper, the shapes of the people are holding hands in a circle - like paper dolls. Practise at home first if you are not sure about how to do this, so that it will be easier to replicate for your group. Provide ready-folded pieces of paper with the outlines drawn on them, together with some pairs of scissors, so that your group can cut out a circle of people themselves.

PRAYER GALLERY

PAPER CIRCLE OF FRIENDSHIP

JIGSAW PUZZLE

Either bring along a ready-made jigsaw puzzle, for people to work on together (a fairly simple one with 40-100 pieces is ideal) or create your own. This can be done by cutting out the large panels from a cereal box, and glueing them together with the printed sides facing each other. This will create a thicker, stronger, plain piece of card to work on. Draw a picture of a heart and colour this in, adding the words 'working together in love'. Cut the puzzle into irregular pieces and place these on a tray so that people can have a go at putting the picture together. Write out this prayer for people to use as they engage with the activity:

'Loving God, thank you that when we work together we see the bigger picture. Amen'

CHAPTER 8
PLAYFULNESS

Enjoy playing some games together as a community and taking part in simple, fun activities, with a reflective and prayerful focus.

BEANBAGS IN A BASKET

Bring along some beanbags (or socks with dry rice inside, tied securely in a knot). Also bring along a box or basket. Mark a place for people to stand with some masking tape (perhaps two places, one for adults and one for children), as well as the position of the box on the floor. People can have a go at throwing the beanbags into the basket. Write out these thoughts for people to reflect on as they take part in the activity:

'As you aim each time and think about where you throw, it (hopefully) gets a little easier and more accurate. Think about what adjustments you need to make to make your throwing more effective. This can be the same in our lives as we practise patience, forgiveness, and kindness each day'

Write out this prayer for people to use, and tape it onto or near the box or basket:

'Lord, thank you for the way you are patient with us, as we learn to live with your love. Help us to be patient with ourselves too. Amen'

JENGA / PICK-UP STICKS

Bring along a tower game, such as Jenga, or a pack of pick-up sticks, and place the game on a tray. Write out this reflection for people to use as they take part in the activity:

'As you take turns to carefully remove a stick or a block, think about the way you need to do this for it to work well. Paying attention, noticing where things are, taking your time, moving slowly and not rushing - these can all be helpful in our prayer too.'

MARBLES / BOULES

Bring along some marbles or a set of boules. If you are using marbles, place them on a piece of carpet or fabric, so that they do not roll everywhere and get lost, or trip people over! The corner of a room could be a good spot for this. Write out these instructions for the activity:

'Take turns rolling the smaller balls as near as you can to the larger target one. Although in the game we can knock others out of the way, we do not need to do this to get close to God. He is always ready to come and find us just where we are.'

FIDGET SPINNER

What these toys are supposed to do is soothe a restless mind and to occupy our hands while our heads tune into a particular task. They aid concentration. Sometimes, however, fidget spinners simply give us something to do with our hands while we essentially do nothing. Provide a few fidget spinners and other fidget toys, and place these near some cushions on the floor for people to sit on. Write out these words as a guide for people engaging in the activity:

'Use the spinner to conscientiously do nothing with God, and to simply be in God's presence, dwelling with God in playfulness. There is no need to come up with lengthy prayers or appear in any way productive. God gives us permission to be intentionally idle in his gentle and loving company.'

PLAYDOUGH

Bring along some playdough for people to spend time shaping, moulding, and squashing. This could either be playdough bought from a shop, or home made. To make homemade playdough, find a large saucepan and add a cup of flour, half a cup of salt, just under a cup of water, a tablespoon of oil, and a teaspoon of cream of tartar. Mix these together, and heat the contents on the stove, stirring all the time. The mixture will become very thick (like an extremely thick white sauce) -- keep stirring, and make sure you scrape along the bottom and sides of the pan. When the mixture has come together into a ball, tip it out onto a working surface and put the pan to soak in cold water. The playdough will be very hot to start with, but as it cools, you can divide it into three or four pieces and knead in some things to make each piece different. This could be food colouring, turmeric powder (for a bright yellow colour), dried camomile (from a couple of camomile tea bags), lavender, cinnamon, mint essence, or vanilla essence. Place the playdough balls on a table with a few cutters and rolling pins. Write out this prayer for people to use as they play with the dough:

'Creator God, thank you for all that you have made. May we use the creativity you have given us to shape the world around us. Amen'

BUILDING TOGETHER

Bring along some Lego bricks or something similar, and tape a large sheet of paper, such as a flipchart page, to a table. On this page, draw a landscape with features such as mountains, a river, a swamp, a volcano, a forest, and a beach. Add a few animals too. People can spend some time together building things that would help others living in the landscape - perhaps a bridge over the river, an ice cream shop by the beach, homes for the animals, or a path across the swamp. Write this prayer on the paper too:

'Lord God, thank you for helping us to use what we have to build a better world. Amen'

CHAPTER 9
REFLECTIONS

An opportunity to think about the way we see ourselves, the way God sees us, and how our lives can reflect God's love in a creative and interactive way.

ICONS TO HELP US THINK

Place some seating so people can sit and look at the biggest wall in your venue. You are going to place some pictures on the wall. Go to the icons on Microsoft Word (or an app of your choice). Search words like: lost, shout, smile, cry, phone, king, friend, letter, thunder, sun, worry, hearing, magnifying glass, book, hello, dead, hold hands, wave, question, talk, jigsaw, compass, wall, punch, breath, door open, door closed, traffic lights. Print these icons on single pieces of paper (perhaps laminate them if you are likely to reuse them in future prayer stations). Alongside these images, print two questions as follows:

'Which of these icons most represents your current relationship to God?'

PRAYER GALLERY

'Which of these icons would you most like to represent your relationship to God?'

Try and fill the wall with as many icons as possible that might conceivably represent someone's interaction with God.

DIFFERENT SHAPED REFLECTIONS

Bring along a few shiny items, for example, some spoons of different sizes, a shiny teapot, some sunglasses, or a stainless steel saucepan. Place these on a table, on a shiny tray or piece of foil, so that people can spend some time looking at their reflections in the different objects. Write out this prayer for people to use as they engage with the exhibit:

'Lord God, thank you for loving us just as we are, however we see ourselves. Thank you that you have created us to be a beautiful and precious reflection of you. Amen'

REFLECTIONS REVEALING BLESSINGS

Using colourful pens, decorate the words of some simple blessings on pieces of paper. You will need to create these in a back-to-front version, so the first step will be to write the words with a soft pencil on a piece of paper in bubble writing. Next, turn the paper face down onto another piece of paper, and use a lolly stick or the back of a pencil to rub over where the lines are, transferring the shape of the words to the other page. Now you can go over these back-to-front words with colourful pens and decorate around them. Use short phrases such as 'God cares for you', 'You are precious', and 'You are loved'. Bring along a mirror or two, preferably without a large frame, so that people can use this to look at the words of blessing and read them, revealed once they take time to look, notice, and reflect.

LANDSCAPE REFLECTIONS

Bring along some pencils, some erasers, and some colouring

pencils, and prepare some colouring sheets for people to use, which show a landscape reflected in water. To make these, fold a piece of A4 paper in half, and either draw, trace, or glue a line drawing of a landscape to the top half, cutting it to size if you are sticking something on. You could find a suitable picture in a colouring book or online. The horizontal fold in the middle of the paper represents the line where the water begins. People can then spend time colouring in the top half of the picture and drawing the 'reflection', upside down in the lower half of the picture. Leave an example for people to see so that they know what to do. Write out this prayer and leave it on the table for people to reflect on as they do their colouring and drawing:

'Holy God, thank you for helping us to reflect some of your kindness, wisdom, and love where we are. May we be ready to look out for your goodness reflected in others too. Amen'

KALEIDOSCOPE REFLECTIONS

For this activity, you will ideally need some mirror card, available online or from craft shops. If you can't get hold of mirror card, some shiny foil, carefully glued and smoothed onto a piece of card (such as a panel from a cereal box), will also work. You will also need some clear plastic, such as the window from some packaging, some sticky tape, and some beads or sequins, as well as some pairs of scissors. First of all, fold your piece of mirror card (or homemade mirror card) into three sections, horizontally. Fold this up, with the shiny side inwards, so that it forms a triangular prism shape, taping the edges in place. Next, cut out two triangles of the plastic packaging window, a little larger than the end of your kaleidoscope. Sandwich a sprinkle of sequins or beads in between the two pieces of plastic and tape securely around the edges so that the small pieces don't fall out. Finally, tape this sparkly triangle onto the end of your kaleidoscope. As you look through the open end and twist the kaleidoscope around, the bright colours will form different patterns in the reflective card. On the outside of the kaleidoscope, write this prayer:

'Lord God, thank you for the love and beauty we see reflected in the world around us. Help us to look out for it wherever we may be. Amen'

MIRROR REFLECTIONS

Bring along a large mirror, and set it up where people can see themselves in it, with some of the rest of the room, the activities, and other community members reflected in it. The idea is that people can look at themselves reflected in the mirror, and see their identity as part of a prayerful and creative community. Write out these phrases on pieces of coloured card, cut them out, and fix them to the edge of the mirror with sticky tack:

'Loved by God'
'Part of a community'
'Creative and prayerful'
'Precious and unique'

Also write out these instructions and fix them to the bottom of the mirror:

'Look at yourself in the mirror, in the context of this place and this community. Remember that you are loved by God and are part of his family as we pray here together. Feel free to take a photo of yourself, reflected in the mirror, as a reminder of this.'

CHAPTER 10
JUSTICE / EQUALITY

Join in some fun and interactive activities to think about the barriers to fairness, justice, and equality, and think prayerfully about how we can make a difference.

PLAYING FAIRLY

Bring along a few games such as pick-up sticks, Jenga, or a pack of cards to build towers from. Bring a couple of pairs of gloves or mittens as well. People can take it in turns to play the games, having a go while wearing gloves and without. Display these questions for people to think about as they play:

'How does it feel playing with the gloves on?
What about when you take them off again?
Would you choose to play with the gloves on?
What would make the games more fair?
How would you feel if you always had to wear the gloves to play the games?'

Next to the questions, display this prayer:

'Lord, help us to notice when things aren't fair, to take action, and to make others aware too. Amen'

TREASURES IN THE SAND

Fill a deep tray with some play sand. In this, at intervals, bury some stones, shells, buttons, beads, pennies, and a few other coins. Have some extras to replace the things with once someone has found them, so that other people can have a go. Write out this prayer as an aid to reflection while people play the game:

'Lord God, in our lives we sometimes have a lot, and sometimes we don't have that much. May we be thankful for what we have and always be ready to share it with others, knowing that it all really belongs to you. Amen'

WORKING TOGETHER FOR JUSTICE

Display some information and pictures from organisations working for justice and equality, such as the Fairtrade Foundation, Traidcraft, Christian Aid, Embrace the Middle East, and Practical Action. Provide scissors, glue, and a large sheet of card so that people can create a collage of actions happening around the world where injustices are being addressed and where people are working towards equality. Write these words of prayer on the card:

'Help us, Lord, as we work together for justice. Amen'

ELEANOR KING & DAN PIERCE

DIFFERENT DRAWINGS

Bring along a few different things to draw with: an old, fat crayon; an artist's pen; a worn out felt-tip; a sharp pencil; a very blunt pencil; a biro pen, a worn out biro, and some watercolour paints, along with both a child's stubby paintbrush and an artist's paintbrush. Provide some pieces of paper for people to draw on and a few simple pictures for them to copy, such as a sunshine, a tree, a cat, and a boat. Write out these instructions for people to follow:

'As you copy the pictures or draw your own, try using some of the different pens, pencils, and paintbrushes provided. Which did you prefer? Which made drawing difficult or even impossible? Use this opportunity to think about the causes of inequality in our community and in our world, and bring these before God in prayer.'

DIFFERENT DRAWINGS

Which pens, pencils and brushes made drawing easy? Which made it difficult?

SONDER

You will need paper and pens for this station. Print the following to accompany it. In 2009, John Koenig began compiling an online lexicon of invented words he called the Dictionary of Obscure Sorrows. He later gained wider recognition in 2016 with a TED talk. In Koenig's imaginative work, he creates words to express emotions, intuitions, and senses that have previously been unnamed, or, in his mind, inadequately named, in the English language. For example, he coined the word Sonder, meaning, the awareness that everyone has a story – that all the random passers-by you see around you have an emotional life just as rich as yours, even though to you they're just an extra in the background.

In German, Sonder is an adjective meaning "special"; in Afrikaans, Sonder means "without." In French, it is a verb meaning "to plumb." So we can perhaps see how Koenig has mixed all these understandings together to come up with his own use of Sonder for English speakers. Along with appreciating the rich individuality of those who fleetingly pass us by, we may experience a further addition to Sonder. That is, it is worth realising God's profound affection for them. Let's call this, to be Sonderful! (If Koenig can invent words, so can we!) This is a love which is not our own but a momentary Divine gift. A love undiluted by man-made demands for religious affiliation or observance. A love undomesticated by reason and science. A love acquainted with yet undeterred by the vivid complexity of anyone's lifes story. A love unsullied by prejudice or cosmetic trivialities. A love to be shown to stranger and enemy.

On a separate instruction sheet, print the following:

'Look around the room at who is there. Draw simple stick-figures around the edge of your own piece of paper to represent each

individual present, without naming them or drawing them in a way that would identify them. For each individual stick-figure, write or think of a single word describing how you honestly (and politely) feel about them. For example, descriptions such as difficult, fun, shy, unapproachable, charismatic, unknown, outgoing, beautiful, awkward, and reliable. Now take some time to Sonder. Think about what you have written or thought about for each one, and allow God to challenge your presuppositions. Pray for each person, 'God help me see this person just as you see them. Fill me with understanding, compassion, respect, grace, and love for this person".

GOD KNOWS ALL OUR NEEDS

If you type 'Maslow's Hierarchy of Needs' into a search engine, you will most likely be confronted with familiar pictures of a colourful, tiered pyramid. Abraham Maslow himself never meant for it to be shown in this way when he submitted his paper; nevertheless, this is how his work is generally presented. The universal needs of society are at its base, proceeding gradually to 'self-actualisation' at the pyramid's pinnacle. In reality, we may revisit these tiers at different times in our lives, perhaps in a more cyclical pattern. For this prayer station, replicate the diagram on the biggest scale you are able using colourful card and clearly marking each tier. Create an accompanying instruction card with a simple description of Maslow's theory as above. Write out these instructions to encourage participants to consider each tier in view of their situation and condition:

'Take a post-it note and write the words 'God is present' on it. Stick this to the pyramid wherever you most need to acknowledge God today. Having done this, you may wish to consider a friend's, neighbour's or family member's situation and add a post-it for them as well.'

CHAPTER 11
LISTENING AND NOTICING

A chance to pay attention using our different senses, through different reflective activities, and to then use this attitude of attentiveness as we listen to God in prayer.

UNIQUE AND BEAUTIFUL

Bring along some stones or shells, or something similar, such as a collection of pine cones, conkers, or leaves. Display these on a flat tray or large plate. Write out these words as an aid to prayer:

'Lord God, your world is full of so many beautiful and different things. As we touch, look at, and arrange the items in front of us, help us to notice and appreciate the uniqueness in each of them, just as you notice the uniqueness in each of us too. Amen'

LISTEN TO THE SEA

Bring along some large shells. Place these on a piece of blue fabric, crumpled to look like the sea. You could add some shiny paper cutout fish to the sea to add to the effect. Write out this prayer for people to use:

'Lord God, as we place the shell to our ear and listen carefully, we can hear a sound like the waves on the seashore. The echoes of the blood in our own bodies, which you have created, sound like the wide ocean. Thank you that we are all a beautiful part of your creation. Amen'

YOGHURT-POT TELEPHONES

Make a few sets of yoghurt pot telephones. Each will need two empty yoghurt pots, hummus tubs, or something similar. Using a blob of sticky tack underneath for safety, make a very small hole carefully in the bottom of each pot with the tip of some small embroidery scissors, a large sewing needle, or a sharp skewer. Cut a 2-3m length of string or embroidery silk and thread this carefully through the hole of one of the pots from underneath. Tie it in a large, strong knot so that the string is secure. Repeat with the other end of the string, threading this through another pot and tying it securely there too. Colour code the telephones, using a different colour string or embroidery silk for each one, and matching the pots to this by glueing tissue paper on the outside.

On the outside of each pot, write some words of blessing in marker pen, such as 'God cares about you', 'You are loved by God', 'You are precious to God', 'You are a child of God', 'God understands' and 'You are God's beautiful creation'. People can then use the telephones in pairs, one person with a pot to their ear, another with a pot to their mouth, with the string tight in between to allow the sound to be heard at the other end, speaking God's words of love and blessing to each other.

CANDLE REFLECTION

Bring along some candles of various shapes and sizes and arrange them safely on a tray filled with sand, perhaps in a corner of the room where it is less likely that a breeze will blow them out. Provide some spaces where people can sit and watch the candles, such as a few cushions on the floor or a piece of carpet to sit on. Light the candles, and write out this prayer for people to use as they spend time watching the candles flicker:

'Loving God, as we watch the candles flickering, bright, and always changing, we thank you for your love that encourages us, strengthens us, helps us, and inspires us. May we always be ready to notice your light in our own lives and in the lives of those around us too. Amen'

MUSICAL JAM JARS

Bring along eight empty glass jam jars of different sizes, some teaspoons, and a large jug filled with water. Place the jars on a tray. By pouring different amounts of water into the jars, different notes can be created when the jars are tapped with the teaspoon. People will need to listen carefully as they add the water to see how much more needs to be poured in or taken out to create the note they want. Through listening, and trial and error, participants can see if they can create a scale of notes using the jars. Write out this prayer and display it next to the jars:

'Lord God, as we listen carefully to the notes the jars create, and respond by adding water or pouring it out, may we learn to listen to you carefully, hour by hour and day by day, adjusting what we do and say in a way that chimes with your values. Amen'

PRAYER SENTENCES

When you know someone intimately, there's a good chance you can end their sentences. That is the relationship we may long for with God — a deep sense of mutual desire and knowing. As we learn to pray, we can learn to pick up with God mid-sentence, to have glimpses of understanding what God may desire in any given situation, and to instinctively long for what God longs for. We can begin to see where God has been and to anticipate how God may be speaking in a situation. Perhaps then we might cautiously open our mouths to harmonise.
Write out these instructions for the activity:

'Prayer is sometimes like being in a jazz quartet with the Trinity... you're all playing different instruments but take turns to play solo. There'll be a chord progression and rhythm to start off with, and then each musician improvises upon the theme. Imagine today that you are joining a jazz quartet in prayer. There are some sentence starters provided; finish the sentence in your own way, improvising as you go:

I wake again because...
The Lord is my....
In my going out and my coming in I will....
Have mercy on me, for I....
My heart is troubled because...
In my hour of disaster, you...
Answer me when I call, Lord, give me....
Let all who take refuge in you...
I have seen sorrows and....
Even though I'm weak, you...
May your blessing be on....
Because of your love, I can...
Be magnified in me so that...
You have shown me....
I am thankful and shout out...
Even when the night draws in, I will praise you because...

CHAPTER 12
CLIMATE AND ENVIRONMENT

A chance to take time to think about the things we treasure in our world, to consider the actions we can take to care for the environment, and to bring all these things in prayer before God.

CARD MATCHING GAME

Create a matching-pairs game of things that people can do to reduce their negative impact on the environment. Cut some card into equally sized squares. On the back of pairs of these, write things such as 'turn the heating down', 'use a hot water bottle', 'walk to places', 'dry washing on a clothes line', 'use a shower timer', 'use up leftover food', 'only buy what you need', 'repair things', 'share lifts', 'refill your water bottle', 'grow your own', 'buy second hand', 'plant a tree' and 'collect rainwater for plants'. Use a different colour pen for each pair so that younger members of the community can be involved in the matching too.

Create another pair of cards with this short prayer on them:

'Lord God, help us to treat your beautiful world with respect and care. Amen.'
Place all the cards face down on a table or on a blanket on the floor so that people can have a go at matching them and thinking about the actions they describe.

PLANT SOME IDEAS

Fill a large tray with compost. Provide some seeds that grow quickly and easily, such as radish, beetroot, or spring onion. Bring along some wooden lolly sticks, some marker pens, some scraps of fabric or colourful paper, some scissors, and some glue sticks. On some of the lolly sticks, write positive actions that people can take to help the environment, such as 'make some compost', 'plant a seed', 'collect up some cans to recycle', 'put out food for the birds', 'plant bee-friendly flowers', 'join in a campaign to help the environment', 'plant a tree', 'join in a beach clean or street clean', and 'make a bug hotel'. Leave some of the lolly sticks blank so that people can write on their own ideas. Write out these instructions for the activity:

'Choose a lolly stick -- either one with words on, or write your own idea. Take a piece of fabric or colourful paper, and cut out a flower shape, using the scissors. Glue this on to the end of your lolly stick. Take a few seeds, make a hole in the compost with your finger and plant them. Next to the seeds, place your decorated ideas stick, to mark the spot. Bring all the good ideas in prayer before God, knowing that he will help both them and the seeds to grow.'

OUR COLOURFUL WORLD

On a large piece of paper or card, such as flipchart paper or an unfolded cardboard box, using a black marker pen or a crayon, draw out an approximate world map. This does not have to be perfect! Use coloured pens or crayons to write the words 'blue' on the ocean area, 'green' on the land area, and 'white' on the arctic and antarctic areas. Bring along some old magazines, advertising flyers, or colourful leaflets, and a few glue sticks. Tear out some of the pages and pictures from the magazines and place them in piles according to their main colour: one pile of blue, one of green, and one white. Write out these instructions for the activity:

'Tear the coloured paper into pieces and glue them onto the picture of the world, according to the colour written there. As you do this, bring that area of the world into God's care, and pray for the animals, plants, and people who live there.'

CLAY CANDLE HOLDERS

Bring along some self hardening clay, some tea lights and some natural objects such as shells, leaves, or stones to make patterns in the clay with. Using an old knife, divide the clay into pieces, keeping them covered until they are ready to be used so that they do not start to dry out. Make a tealight holder as an example, and write out these instructions for people to follow:

'Take a tealight and a piece of clay. Press the tealight into the clay and squash the clay around the side to create a holder shape. Smooth the sides with your fingers, and press the clay onto a smooth surface to create a flat base. When your tealight holder is the shape you would like it to be, decorate it by carefully pressing stones, shells, and leaves into the clay. Leave your tealight holder to dry. At home, find a time in the evening to light the candle, turn off all the other lights in the house, and spend some time in God's presence, praying for and giving thanks for our beautiful world.'

ELEANOR KING & DAN PIERCE

LOVE IT, DON'T WASTE IT

LOVE IT, DON'T WASTE IT

Create a pile of broken bits of furniture or electrical appliances. Make it look messy and discarded. Then present the following text on a card next to it to explain the installation.
'Hundreds of thousands of items of furniture get dumped in landfill every year – a sign of how out of balance our consumption has become. We have a tendency to want more than we actually need and struggle to determine what is 'enough.' However, what we use, what we own, and what we discard should be part of our life of prayer. Our possessions and waste must be subject to prayerful consideration.
Sitting and looking at this installation, think about your own 'stuff'. Ponder your recent or planned purchases and pray.'
Write out the following helpful words as an aid to prayer and reflection:

'Creator God, help us know our limits. Help us be grateful for what we have and mindful of what we use. Make us responsible stewards of your creation so that we can find satisfaction and contentment in you. May we make our choices in the light of your grace and wisdom. Amen'

ENDANGERED SPECIES IN THE BALANCE

On the website worldwildlife.org, there is a Species Directory that shows the conservation status of hundreds of animals. Print and present a list of all the animals that are critically endangered, endangered, vulnerable, and near-threatened. Find some soft toys that resemble some of the animals on the list and tape them around the edge of a basket or bucket. Set up a simple seesaw (such as a plank of wood balanced on a brick) and tape the basket of teddies securely to one end. Tape another similar basket or bucket in place on the other end of the seesaw, with a sign on it that says 'EXTINCTION!' Put some stones inside it so that this end of the seesaw is heavier. Provide some permanent marker pens so that people can take a stone out of the 'extinction' bin, write a prayer of hope on it, and place it carefully into the basket of teddies. As people do this, the prayers will tip the balance so that the teddies' end is now heavier.

On a piece of card, write the following prayer and stick it to the bin below the sign:

'Lord of all life. We thank you for the wonder of creation. Wake us up to the great harm we cause to the things you have made. Turn our concern and our tears at the irreversible loss of wildlife and habitat into solid action. Move our hearts, move our hands, our wallets, our pens, our will, and our creativity to help prevent further extinction and destruction of this sacred planet. Amen'

PRAYER GALLERY

ENDANGERED SPECIES IN THE BALANCE

WRITE A PRAYER ON A STONE, AND PLACE IT IN THE BASKET OF TEDDIES TO TIP THE BALANCE